W9-BMY-941

Half or Whole?

Susan Markowitz Meredith

www.rourkepublishing.com

www.rourkepublishing.com

PHOTO CREDITS: Cover: © Nicole S. Young; Title Page: © Ekaterina Monakhova; Page 3: © Geoffrey Black, © Boris Terekhov; Page 4: © Geoffrey Black; Page 5: © Boris Terekhov; Page 7, 11: © Shiffti, © Kelly Cline, © DNY59; Page 8, 13: © Kelly Cline; Page 9, 12: © Shiffti, © DNY59; Page 10: © Matthew Heinrichs; Page 15, 19: © Guillermo Lobo, © Yong Hian Lim, © kutay tanir, © Robert Kacpura; Page 16, 20: © kutay tanir; Page 17: © © Guillermo Lobo, © Robert Kacpura; Page 18: © Edyta Grabowska; Page 22: © Fertnig; Page 23: © DNY59

Edited by Kelli L. Hicks

Cover and Interior design by Tara Raymo

Library of Congress Cataloging-in-Publication Data

Meredith, Susan, 1951-
 Half or whole? / Susan Markowitz Meredith.
    p. cm. -- (Little world math concepts)
 Includes bibliographical references and index.
 ISBN 978-1-61590-293-4 (Hard Cover) (alk. paper)
 ISBN 978-1-61590-532-4 (Soft Cover)
 1. Fractions--Juvenile literature. 2. Number concept--Juvenile literature. I. Title.
 QA117.M37 2011
 513.2'6--dc22
                              2010009896

Rourke Publishing
Printed in the United States of America, North Mankato, Minnesota
033010
033010LP

www.rourkepublishing.com - rourke@rourkepublishing.com
Post Office Box 643328 Vero Beach, Florida 32964

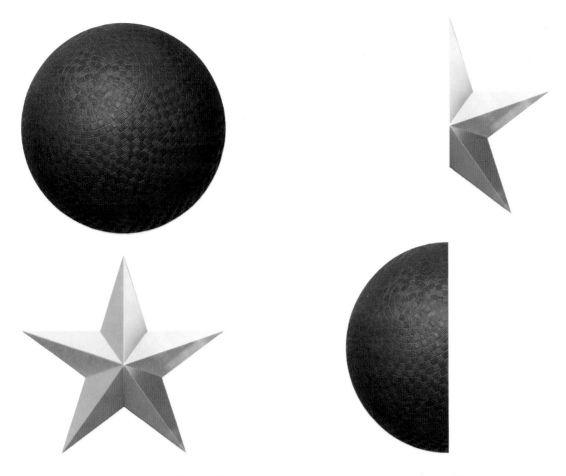

Half and whole, can you tell them apart?

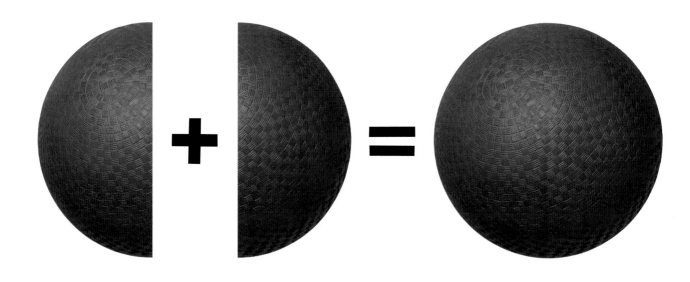

Two halves make a whole.

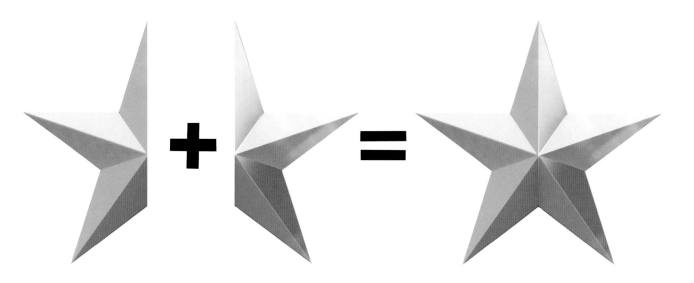

That's a good start.

Are these half sandwiches?
Or are they whole ones?

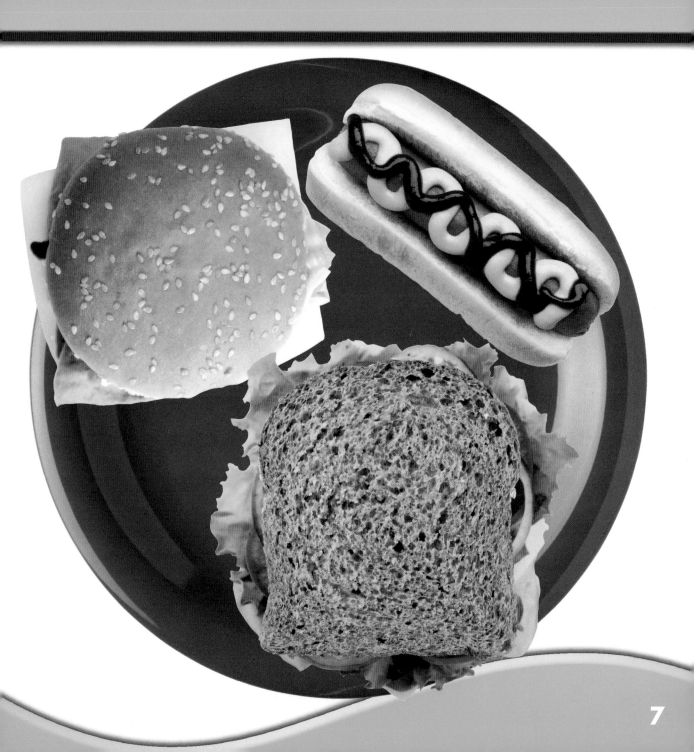

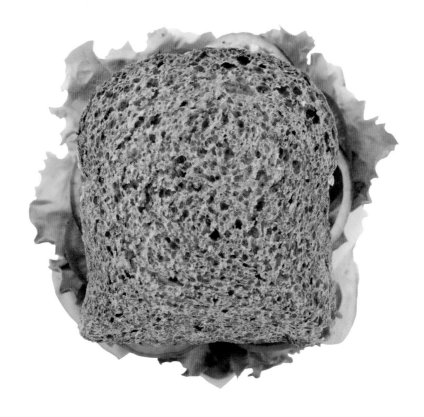

The sandwiches are whole.

See the shapes of the buns?

Cut them all in two parts.

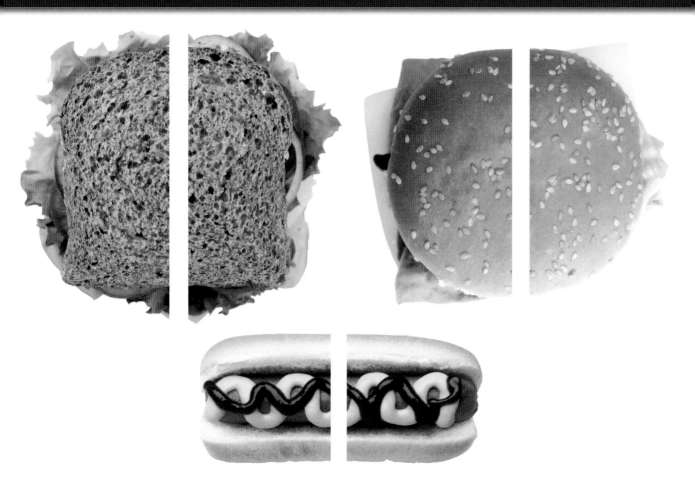

Both are the same size.

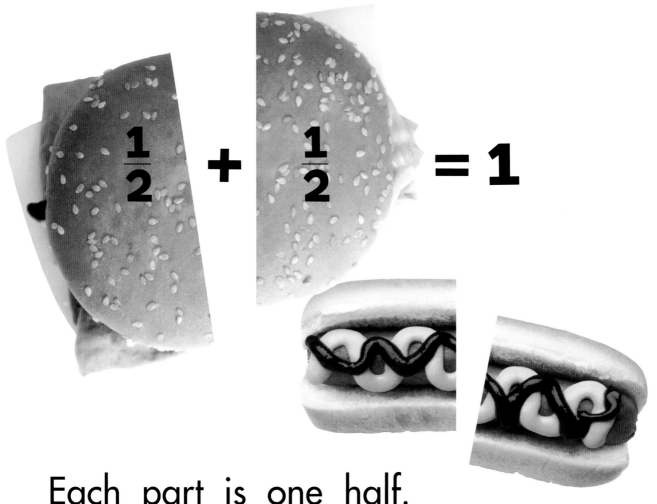

$\frac{1}{2}$ + $\frac{1}{2}$ = 1

Each part is one half.

No surprise!

Are these fruits whole?
Or do you see a half here?

These fruits are whole.

A banana, apple, and pear.

Cut them all in two parts.

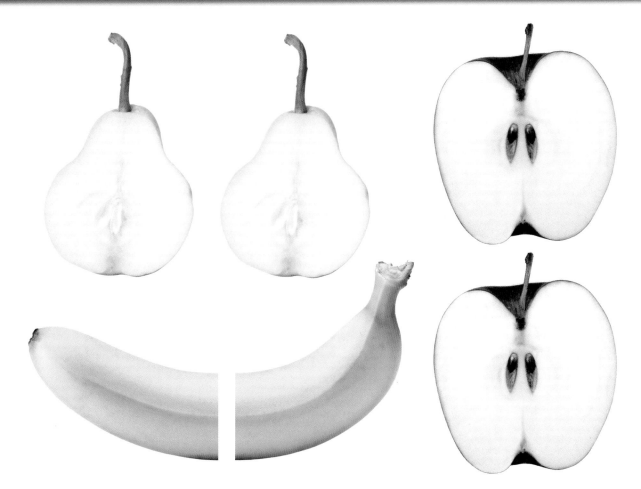

Both are the same size.

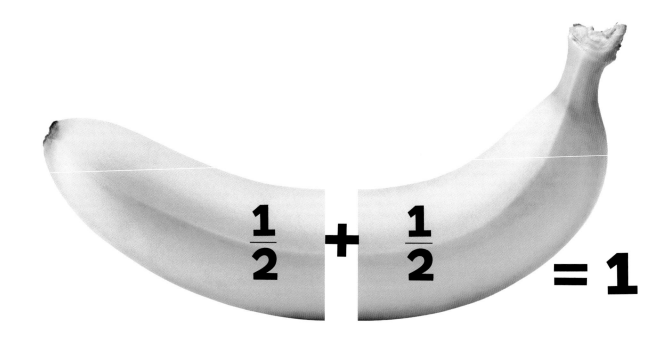

$$\frac{1}{2} + \frac{1}{2} = 1$$

Each part is one half.

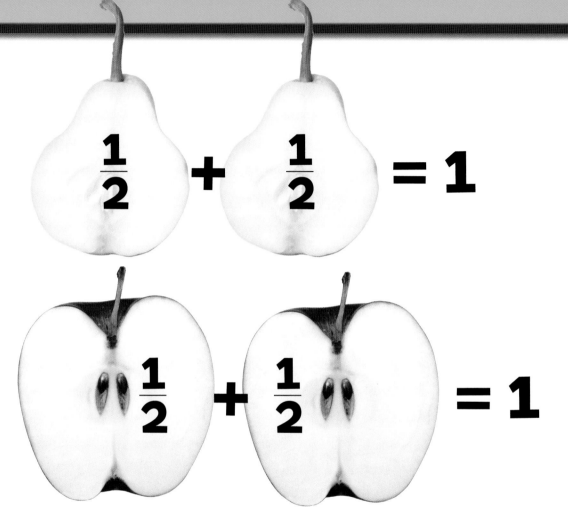

$$\frac{1}{2} + \frac{1}{2} = 1$$

$$\frac{1}{2} + \frac{1}{2} = 1$$

No surprise!

Half or whole, what do you see?

Index

Websites

www.pbskids.org/cyberchase/games/fractions/index.html

www.beaconlearningcenter.com/weblessons/iwantmyhalf/default.htm

www.macmillanmh.com/math/2003/student/activity/courses/grk/ch10b

About the Author

Susan Markowitz Meredith likes to make tasty treats in her home in New York City. Her recipes call for many ingredients in different amounts. She is glad to know the difference between half and whole.